Math Mammoth
Grade 6
Skills Review Workbook
Answer Key

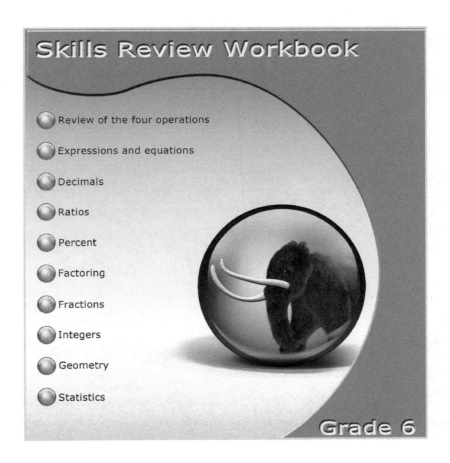

By Maria Miller

Contents

Chapter 1: Review of the Basic Operations

Skills Review 1, p. 7

1. a. $7^6 = 117,649$ b. $9^4 = 6,561$
   c. $80^2 = 6,400$ d. $60^3 = 216,000$

2. 2,415 R21; $39 \times 2,415 + 21 = 94,206$

3. $1/8 + 2/3 = 3/24 + 16/24 = 19/24$. So, 5/24 of the students ride to school in cars.

4. a. $5,240 - 140 \times 30 = 5,240 - 4,200 = \underline{1,040}$
   b. $975 + 80 = \underline{1,055}$

5. $86 = 2 \times 43$

6.

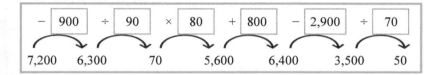

	900	÷	90	×	80	+	800	−	2,900	÷	70

7,200   6,300   70   5,600   6,400   3,500   50

Skills Review 2, p. 8

1. a.

Miles	12 mi	24 mi	36 mi	72 mi	144 mi	180 mi	216 mi
Time	10 min	20 min	30 min	1 hour	2 hours	2 1/2 hours	3 hours

b. The train will travel $72 \times 8 = 576$ miles in 8 hours.

c. Students' estimates will vary. It will take about 7 hours for the train to travel 465 miles.

2. a. 4 b. 9 c. 7 d. 3 e. 9 f. 120

3.

	34,880	

15,370	19,510

6,260	9,110	10,400

2,870	3,390	5,720	4,680

4.
```
        7 3 5
  x     2 0 8
      5 8 8 0
      0 0 0
  1 4 7 0
  1 5 2,8 8 0
```

5. Susan got 20 full bottles of juice. One gallon is 4 quarts, and one quart is 4 cups, so two gallons is $2 \times 4 \times 4 = 32$ cups. After drinking one cup, she had 31 cups of juice. Each cup is 8 ounces, so 31 cups is $31 \times 8 = 248$ ounces. We divide that by 12 to get the number of bottles: $248 \div 12 = 20$ R8, which means she got 20 full bottles of juice, and 8 oz left over.

6. a. 7,004,002 b. 30,850,900

Skills Review 3, p. 9

1.

Number	514,372	827,491	36,594,136	7,091,512	4,978,627
...thousand	514,000	827,000	36,594,000	7,092,000	4,979,000
...ten thousand	510,000	830,000	36,590,000	7,090,000	4,980,000
...hundred thousand	500,000	800,000	36,600,000	7,100,000	5,000,000
...million	1,000,000	1,000,000	37,000,000	7,000,000	5,000,000

2. a. $=$ b. $<$ c. $<$
   d. $>$ e. $<$ f. $>$

3.

$8^1 = 8$
$8^2 = 64$
$8^3 = 512$
$8^4 = 4,096$
$8^5 = 32,768$
$8^6 = 262,144$

4. a. $57 \div 9 = 6$ R3; $9 \times 6 + 3 = 57$ b. $71 \div 6 = 11$ R5; $6 \times 11 + 5 = 71$

5. a. $A = 8 \text{ km} \times 8 \text{ km} = 64 \text{ km}^2$ b. $A = 11 \text{ m} \times 11 \text{ m} = 121 \text{ m}^2$

Puzzle Corner. There could also be other solutions.

$\frac{1}{4}$	$+$	$\frac{5}{12}$	$=\frac{16}{24}$	$\frac{3}{10}$	$+$	$\frac{1}{3}$	$=\frac{19}{30}$
$+$		$+$		$+$		$+$
$\frac{2}{9}$	$+$	$\frac{2}{5}$	$=\frac{28}{45}$	$\frac{2}{7}$	$+$	$\frac{5}{8}$	$=\frac{51}{56}$
$=$		$=$		$=$		$=$
$\frac{17}{36}$		$\frac{49}{60}$		$\frac{41}{70}$		$\frac{23}{24}$

Skills Review 4, p. 10

1.

a. $3,580 \times 21,040$
  Estimation: $4,000 \times 21,000 = 84,000,000$
  or $4,000 \times 20,000 = 80,000,000$
  or $3,500 \times 20,000 = 70,000,000$
  Exact: $3,580 \times 21,040 = 75,323,200$
  Error of estimation: 8,676,800 or 4,676,800 or 5,323,200
	b. $48,732 \div 4,216$
	  Estimation: $48,000 \div 4,000 = 12$
	  Exact: $48,732 \div 4,216 = 11.56$
	  Error of estimation: 0.44

2. The cheaper fabric costs $7.45 \div 5 \times 3 = \$4.47$ a yard. Brenna paid $4 \times \$7.45 + 7 \times \$4.47 = \$61.09$.
   She has $\$90 - \$61.09 = \$28.91$ left after buying the fabric.

3. a. 40   b. 8   c. 350   d. 38   e. 16

4. a. 93.24   b. 8.7

5. a. 0.9   b. 0.9   c. 7

Chapter 2: Expressions and Equations

Skills Review 5, p. 11

1. a. 5.46 km

5.	4	6				
km	hm	dam	m	dm	cm	mm

b. 39.8 dm

			3	9.	8	
km	hm	dam	m	dm	cm	mm

c. 5.46 km = __54.6__ hm = __546__ dam = __5,460__ m

39.8 dm = __3.98__ m = __0.398__ dam = __0.0398__ hm

2.

a.	$\dfrac{56}{7} \cdot 6 = 48$	b.	$\dfrac{81}{9 \cdot 3} \cdot 12 = 36$	c.	$6 \cdot \dfrac{8}{4} \cdot 5 = 60$

3. The total area of the building is 528 ft².

$22 \text{ ft} \times 12 \text{ ft} + 10 \text{ ft} \times 12 \text{ ft} + 12 \text{ ft} \times 12 \text{ ft} = 264 \text{ ft}^2 + 120 \text{ ft}^2 + 144 \text{ ft}^2 = 528 \text{ ft}^2$

4. a. $V = 7 \text{ cm} \times 7 \text{ cm} \times 7 \text{ cm} = 343 \text{ cm}^3$

b. $V = 4 \text{ m} \times 4 \text{ m} \times 4 \text{ m} = 64 \text{ m}^3$

5.

a. $7\dfrac{4}{9} - 2\dfrac{6}{15}$	b. $9\dfrac{7}{12} + 14\dfrac{3}{8}$
$\downarrow \qquad \downarrow$	$\downarrow \qquad \downarrow$
$7\dfrac{20}{45} - 2\dfrac{18}{45} = 5\dfrac{2}{45}$	$9\dfrac{14}{24} + 14\dfrac{9}{24} = 23\dfrac{23}{24}$

Skills Review 6, p. 12

1. a. $x = 5{,}600$ b. $M = 90$

2. a. 3 2/3   b. 36/60   c. 12/15   d. 4 7/28

3. a. 2,780,000; 2,820,000; 2,860,000; 2,900,000; 2,940,000; 2,980,000; 3,020,000; 3,060,000; 3,100,000

b. 923,752; 923,452; 923,152; 922,852; 922,552; 922,252; 921,952; 921,652; 921,352

4.
```
      $ 6 5 . 3 8
    ×         4 7
      4 5 7 6 6
    2 6 1 5 2
  $ 3 , 0 7 2 . 8 6
```

5.

9	14	13	16
42	44	32	27
12	18	41	22
5	21	11	17
15	7	8	26
36	28	40	33
24	10	3	29

6. a. They receive about 3,000 e-mails in three weeks. First, find the approximate number of e-mails that they receive in one day: Damian receives about $90 \div 3 \times 2 = 60$; Stella receives about $60 \div 4 \times 3 = 45$. In total, they three receive about $90 + 60 + 45 = 195 \approx 200$ emails in a day, and $200 \times 5 = 1{,}000$ emails in a week. In three weeks, they receive therefore about $1{,}000 \times 3 = 3{,}000$ emails.

b. They receive about 49,000 e-mails in 49 weeks.

7.

a. $\dfrac{480}{8} + \dfrac{64}{8} = 60 + 8 = 68$	b. $\dfrac{540}{6} + \dfrac{60}{6} - \dfrac{18}{6} = 90 + 10 - 3 = 97$	c. $\dfrac{160}{5} - \dfrac{70}{5} = 32 - 14 = 18$

Skills Review 7, p. 13

1. a. $3 \times 9 + 26 = 27 + 26 = 53$
   b. $32 \div 8 \times 15 = 4 \times 15 = 60$

2. a. The lamps that Mariah bought originally cost $42 \div 2 \times 3 = \$63$ each. The lamps that Shelly bought originally cost $45 \div 3 \times 5 = \$75$ each. Note: The student can also draw bar models to help with solving this problem.

   b. At the original price, Mariah would have paid $3 \times \$63 = \$189$, and Shelly would have paid $3 \times 75 = \$225$. At the discounted price, Mariah paid $3 \times \$42 = \$126$, and Shelly paid $3 \times \$45 = \$135$. Mariah saved $\$189 - \$126 = \$63$, and Shelly saved $\$225 - \$135 = \$90$. So, Shelly saved $\$90 - \$63 = \$27$ more than Mariah.

Find the original price of each kind of lamp.
↓
Find the total cost that each girl would pay if they bought the lamps at the original price.
↓
Find the total cost that each girl pays for the lamps at the discounted price.
↓
Subtract the total discounted price that each girl paid from the total original price.
↓
Subtract the lower discounted price from the higher discounted price..

3. Kyle will spend approximately $4,000 on rental fees in a year.
   In a month, he spends about $\$60 \times 3 \times 2 = \$360$. In a year, he spends about $\$360 \times 12 \approx \$400 \times 10 = \$4,000$.

4. a. 217; Check: $44 \times 217 = 9,548$
   b. 0.438; Check: $60 \times 0.438 = 26.28$

Skills Review 8, p. 14

1. a. If the square's area is 81 cm^2, then the length of one side is 9 cm. So the perimeter is 4×9 cm $= 36$ cm.
   b. Since $5^3 = 5 \times 5 \times 5 = 125$, a cube with a volume of 125 in^3 has sides that are 5 in. long.

2. a. $\frac{13}{4} \times \frac{9}{5} = \frac{117}{20} = 5\frac{17}{20}$. Estimate: $3 \times 2 = 6$.

   b. $\frac{8}{5} \times \frac{10}{3} = \frac{8}{1} \times \frac{2}{3} = \frac{16}{3} = 5\frac{1}{3}$. Estimate: $1\frac{1}{2} \times 3 = 4\frac{1}{2}$.

3. a. $2x + x = 3x$ b. $2z + 18$

4.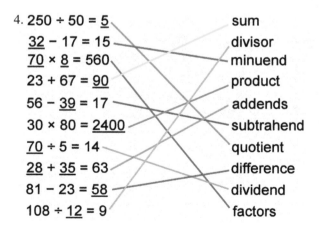

   250 ÷ 50 = 5 .... sum
   32 − 17 = 15 .... divisor
   70 × 8 = 560 .... minuend
   23 + 67 = 90 .... product
   56 − 39 = 17 .... addends
   30 × 80 = 2400 .... subtrahend
   70 ÷ 5 = 14 .... quotient
   28 + 35 = 63 .... difference
   81 − 23 = 58 .... dividend
   108 ÷ 12 = 9 .... factors

5. a. 1,600   b. 130   c. 227   d. 2,500

Skills Review 9, p. 15

1. a. $y + 18$ b. $10p$ c. $7x$

2. a. $21/7 = \underline{3}$
   b. $70 + 9 \cdot 30 - 45 = 70 + 270 - 45 = \underline{295}$
   c. $12 + 125 = \underline{137}$

3. a. 256.67   b. 57.778

4. a. $10^8 < 180{,}000{,}000 < 8{,}000{,}000{,}000$ b. $5 \times 10^7 < 350{,}000{,}000 < 3 \times 10^9$

5. Brandon paid approximately $230 + $180 + 2 \times $25 = $460.
   Exact cost: $453.98

6.

a. $8 \cdot 397 = 8 \cdot (400 - 3)$ $= \underline{3{,}200 - 24 = 3{,}176}$	b. $6 \cdot 7{,}050 = 6 \cdot (7{,}000 + 50)$ $= \underline{42{,}000 + 300 = 42{,}300}$

Skills Review 10, p. 16

1.

a. $8(30 + 7) = 8 \cdot 30 + 8 \cdot 7 = 240 + 56 = 296$	b. $5(s + 9) = 5 \cdot s + 5 \cdot 9 = 5s + 45$
c. $z(50 + x) = z \cdot 50 + z \cdot x = 50z + xz$	d. $7(3a + 6b) = 21a + 42b$

2. a. $\underline{13}$ < $\underline{14}$ < $\underline{15}$ < $\underline{16}$
       prime   multiple of 7   factor of 45   square number

   b. $\underline{27}$ < $\underline{28}$ < $\underline{29}$ < $\underline{30}$
       cube number   multiple of 4   prime   factor of 120

3. a. $50(x - 230)$

   b. $\dfrac{84 + x}{9}$

   c. $y - \dfrac{300}{60}$

4. First, find the cost of an apple pie: $42 \div 3 \times 2 = $28. Then, find the
   total cost of the cheesecakes and pies: $2 \times $42 + 3 \times $28 = $168.

5. a. $A = 20x^2$ $P = 18x$ b. $A = 18y^2$ $P = 18y$

Skills Review 11, p. 17

1. a. 82   b. 540   c. 70

2. a. Equation: $x - 36 = 487$ Solution: $x = 523$
   b. Equation: $7x = 105$ Solution: $x = 15$
   c. Equation: $x \div 9 = 14$ Solution: $x = 126$

3.

Number	7,632,948,173	15,190,705,214	4,578,213,697	9,413,582,301
...ten million	7,630,000,000	15,190,000,000	4,580,000,000	9,410,000,000
...hundred million	7,600,000,000	15,200,000,000	4,600,000,000	9,400,000,000
...billion	8,000,000,000	15,000,000,000	5,000,000,000	9,000,000,000

4. a. He drives 7.5 miles in 10 minutes. Ten minutes is 1/6 of an hour, so we divide
   Richard's speed per hour by six to find the answer: $45 \div 6 = 7.5$
   b. Answers will vary. Check the student's answer. For example: it would take him approximately $600 \div 50 = 12$ hours to
   drive 600 miles.

5.

a. $4x + 7$	b. $2y + 4p$ or $4p + 2y$
c. $6s$	d. $31x + 5y$

Skills Review 12, p. 18

1. The variables (letters) that students choose will vary.
   a. $s \le \$12$ b. $a \ge 16$ c. $g < 10$

2. a. $7^8 = 5,764,801$ b. $4^6 = 4,096$

3.

a. $7,325 = 7000 + 300 + 20 + 5$ $= 7 \times 10^3 + 3 \times 10^2 + 2 \times 10^1 + 5 \times 10^0$	b. $12,800 = 10,000 + 2,000 + 800$ $= 1 \times 10^4 + 2 \times 10^3 + 8 \times 10^2$
c. $2,400,703 = 2,000,000 + 400,000 + 700 + 3$ $= 2 \times 10^6 + 4 \times 10^5 + 7 \times 10^2 + 3 \times 10^0$	

4. a. $12p \cdot 12p = 144p^2$ b. $6 \cdot 7x = 42x$

5.

a.	b.	c.
$3y + 4y = 35$ $7y = 35 \mid \div 7$ $y = 5$	$12x - 3x = 72$ $9x = 72 \mid \div 9$ $x = 8$	$7a + 4a - 3a = 48$ $8a = 48 \mid \div 8$ $a = 6$

6. Marilyn originally had $5,840 in savings. $\$4,380 \div 3 \times 4 = \$5,840$

1. a. $7(6 + a + b + 5) = 77 + 7a + 7b$ b. $4(y + 9 + r) = 4y + 36 + 4r$

2.

x	2	3	4	5	6	7
y	1	3	5	7	9	11

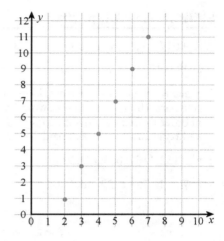

3. Each one paid $5 \times \$180 \div 4 = \underline{\$225}$.

4. Eric's vegetable garden has an area of 360 ft^2.
   To find the answer, subtract the area of Eric's flower garden
   from the total area of his garden: 450 ft^2 − 90 ft^2 = 360 ft^2

5. a. $73 \div 8 = 9$ R1; $8 \times 9 + 1 = 73$
   b. $87 \div 12 = 7$ R3; $7 \times 12 + 3 = 87$

6. a. 579 b. 286

Chapter 3: Decimals

Skills Review 14, p. 20

1. a. 9.017   b. 0.58   c. 5.002641   d. 0.0083

2. a. $40 - 17 - 9 = 14$ b. $40 + (17 - 9) = 48$

3. Since Kyle and Justin each paid twice as much as Liam, you can divide the price into five parts (by five) to find how much Liam paid. Then, multiply that amount by two in order to find out how much Kyle and Justin paid. Liam paid $7,960 ÷ 5 = $1,592, and Kyle and Justin each paid 2 × $1,592 = $3,184.

4. a. 5,152,446   b. 3,173,296

5. a. 70   b. 7.   c. 32   d. 900

6.

Expression	The terms in it	Coefficient(s)	Constants
$y \cdot 5$	$y \cdot 5$	5	none
$7x^2y^6 + 12$	$7x^2y^6$ and 12	7	12
$\frac{16}{29}y$	$\frac{16}{29}y$	$\frac{16}{29}$	none

Skills Review 15, p. 21

1.

a. $248,341 - 12 \times 3,127$ Estimation: $250,000 - 10 \times 3,000 = 220,000$ or $250,000 - 12 \times 3,000 = 214,000$ Exact: $248,341 - 12 \times 3,127 = 210,817$ Error of estimation: 9,183 or 3,183	b. $34,542 ÷ 731$ Estimation: $35,000 ÷ 700 = 50$ Exact: $34,542 ÷ 731 = 47.3$ Error of estimation: 2.7

2. a. No.   b. The root is 72: 72/6 = 12.

3. a. $0.00089 < 0.0024 < 0.12$ b. $2.00999 < 2.069 < 2.692$

4. a. <u>348</u> 12 ⑧ 29 ⑨ 58
   b. <u>123</u> ⑯ ⑦ ㊳ ㉓ ④
   c. <u>580</u> ⑥ 116 5 ㉗ 20

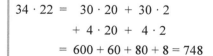

5.

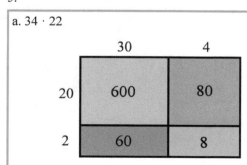

a. $34 \cdot 22$

$34 \cdot 22 = 30 \cdot 20 + 30 \cdot 2$
$+ 4 \cdot 20 + 4 \cdot 2$
$= 600 + 60 + 80 + 8 = 748$

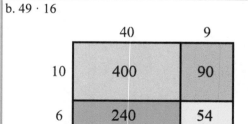

b. $49 \cdot 16$

$49 \cdot 16 = 40 \cdot 10 + 40 \cdot 6$
$+ 9 \cdot 10 + 9 \cdot 6$
$= 400 + 240 + 90 + 54 = 784$

12

Skills Review 16, p. 22

1. a. 3.82982   b. 20.148536

2. a. $8 \cdot (70 - 30) + 20 = 340$ b. $(84 + 6) \div 6 - 15 = 0$ c. $(260 - (80 + 50)) \div 5 = 26$

3. Each one paid $347.50. $(2 \times \$465 + \$7,410) \div 24 = \$347.50$

4. a. $16y + 3$ b. $16p^2$ c. $6m + 8n$ d. $27y + 3x + 2$ or $3x + 27y + 2$

5. a.   <u> 64 </u> < <u> 65 </u> < <u> 66 </u> < <u> 67 </u>
      cube number   multiple of 13   multiple of 6   prime

   b.   <u> 78 </u> < <u> 79 </u> < <u> 80 </u> < <u> 81 </u>
      multiple of 26   prime   factor of 320   square number

6.

a. $7^4 = 2,401$	b. $5^6 = 15,625$	c. $8^7 = 2,097,152$
$4^8 = 65,536$	$9^4 = 6,561$	$10^9 = 1,000,000,000$

Skills Review 17, p. 23

1.

| a. 3.73916 + 0.4652
  Estimate: 3.7 + 0.5 = 4.2

Exact: 3.7 3 9 1 6
      +0.4 6 5 2
      ⎯⎯⎯⎯⎯⎯
      4.2 0 4 3 6 | b. 7.695218 − 1.408361
  Estimate: 7.7 − 1.4 = 6.3

Exact: 7.6 9 5 2 1 8
      −1.4 0 8 3 6 1
      ⎯⎯⎯⎯⎯⎯
      6.2 8 6 8 5 7 |

2. a. 283   b. 537   c. 40

3. a. $65 + 18 \frac{1}{2} = x$ or $x - 18 \frac{1}{2} = 65$; $x = 83 \frac{1}{2}$. Beth will be 83 ½ when Seth is 65.
   b. $32v = \$272$; $v = \$8.50$. One vase costs $8.50.

4.

a. $4x + 4 = 4(x + 1)$	b. $5y + 15 = 5(y + 3)$
c. $7x + 35 = 7(x + 5)$	d. $9x + 18y + 36 = 9(x + 2y + 4)$

Skills Review 18, p. 24

1.

| a. $0.54 \div 6 = 0.09$
$6 \times 0.09 = 0.54$ | b. $7.2 \div 8 = 0.9$
$8 \times 0.9 = 7.2$ | c. $0.009 \div 3 = 0.003$
$3 \times 0.003 = 0.009$ | d. $0.00096 \div 12 = 0.00008$
$12 \times 0.00008 = 0.00096$ |

2. Estimates will vary. For example: $\$1,500 \times 60 = \$90,000$.
   Exact: $\$1,475 \times 64 = \$94,400$.

3. a. $A = 20x^2$ $P = 24x$ b. $A = 114p^2$ $P = 46p$

4. a. 641/100,000   b. 9752/1,000,000   c. 30,039/10,000

5.

a. $x < 3$

b. $x \geq 29$

Skills Review 19, p. 25

1. a. 0.012 b. 0.343 c. 0.00216 d. 0.00064

2. a. $\dfrac{8x-4}{6}$ or $(8x-4) \div 6$ b. $(9+x)^3$ c. $7(x+5)$ d. $2(3+x+7)$

3. a.

x	0	2	4	6	8	10
y	1	3	5	7	9	11

b.

x	3	4	5	6	7	8	9	10
y	0	1	2	3	4	5	6	7

Equation: $y = x + 1$

Equation: $y = x - 3$

4. Cassandra had $228.13 left.

5. a. $110 + 225 = 335$ b. $600 + 90 = 690$

Skills Review 20, p. 26

1. a. $7.1 \div 6 \approx 1.183$ b. $3 \div 11 \approx 0.273$ c. $8.5 \div 3 \approx 2.833$

2.

Number	3,975,491,872	9,184,702,537	19,963,261,583
...ten million	3,980,000,000	9,180,000,000	19,960,000,000
...hundred million	4,000,000,000	9,200,000,000	20,000,000,000
...billion	4,000,000,000	9,000,000,000	20,000,000,000

3. Answers will vary. Please check the student's answers. For example:
   a. 2.468 b. 7.265 c. 5.07 d. 3.648

4.

numbers/letters	sum	difference	product	quotient
a. 24 and 6	30	18	144	4
b. p and x	$p+x$	$p-x$	px	$\dfrac{p}{x}$

Puzzle Corner:

a. $\dfrac{480-7}{10} = 48 - \dfrac{7}{10}$

b. $\dfrac{31-6}{7} = 4\dfrac{3}{7} - \dfrac{6}{7}$

Skills Review 21, p. 27

1. a. $70^2 = 4,900$ b. $5^5 = 3,125$

2. a. $4.7 + 0.82 = 5.52$ b. $0.4 + 0.57 = 0.97$ c. $5.49 + 0.3 = 5.79$ d. $8.953 - 0.4 = 8.553$

3.

a. $230 + 80 = 310$	b. $49 \cdot 125 = 6,125$	c. $480 \div 6 \cdot 10,000 = 800,000$

4. The average is the sum of all the ages of the fire-fighters divided by the total number of fire-fighters:
   $(28 + 20 + 25 + 24 + 19 + 23 + 32 + 18 + 26 + 30 + 27 + 29 + 31 + 22 + 34) \div 15 \approx 26$.

5. Frank drives $28.6 \times 5 \times 3 = 429$ km in three weeks.

6. a. $21x + 5$ b. $22z^7$ c. $m + 20n$ d. $19p + 3s + 4$

7. a. $x = 2,400$ b. $M = 140$ c. $y = 460$

14

Skills Review 22, p. 28

1.

a. $6\frac{24}{40} = 6\frac{6}{10} = 6.6$	b. $\frac{35}{500} = \frac{7}{100} = 0.07$	c. $4\frac{1}{4} = 4\frac{25}{100} = 4.25$

2. a. 99,825,000 b. 40,847,900

3.

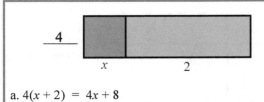 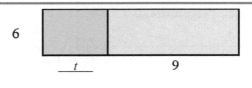

a. $4(x + 2) = 4x + 8$	b. $6(t + 9) = 6t + 54$

4.

Number:	0.470582	8.095326	1.5276301	0.853109	3.472635
…three decimals	0.471	8.095	1.528	0.853	3.473
…five decimals	0.47058	8.09533	1.52763	0.85311	3.47264

5. a. The root is 5: $5^3 + 16 - 2 \cdot 5 = 131$.
   b. The root is 4: $5 \cdot 4 - 8 = 3 \cdot 4$.

6. a. $4 \times 6 + 39 = 24 + 39 = 63$ b. $\frac{72}{9} \times 15 = 8 \times 15 = 120$

Skills Review 23, p. 29

1. They spent $954 on groceries in May, and $1,146 in June. To find how much
   they spent in May, first subtract from the total amount the $192 more that they
   spent in June, and then divide what is left by two: ($2,100 − $192) ÷ 2 = $954.
   Then, to find how much they spent in June, simply add $192 to the amount that
   they spent in May: $954 + $192 = $1,146.

2. a. 0.0049; 0.26
   b. 83,542; 31,950
   c. 4,273,000; 8,038,160

3. Answers will vary. Please check the student's work. Examples:
   a. The game costs less than $30.
   b. Buy at least 14 apples.
   c. There will be more than 150 people attending the seminar.

4. Each one paid $41. $246 ÷ 6 = $41

5. In these, one way to solve them is to first find half of the perimeter. Then it is easy to find the other side, since
   the two sides add up to the half of the perimeter.
   a. 11x b. 15s

15

Skills Review 24, p. 30

1. a. 23.8 b. 205.9

2.

a.				
$4x + 5x$	=	$46 - 19$		
$9x$	=	27		$\div 9$
x	=	3		

b.			
$9c - c$	=	$2 \cdot 60$	
$8c$	=	120	$\div 8$
c	=	15	

c.			
$33x - 8x + 3x$	=	$14 \cdot 60$	
$28x$	=	840	$\div 28$
x	=	30	

3.

a. $0.7 \times 0.05 = 0.035$

$$\frac{7}{10} \times \frac{5}{100} = \frac{35}{1000}$$

b. $0.006 \times 0.9 = 0.0054$

$$\frac{6}{1000} \times \frac{9}{10} = \frac{54}{10,000}$$

c. $0.012 \times 0.0008 = 0.0000096$

$$\frac{12}{1000} \times \frac{8}{10,000} = \frac{96}{10,000,000}$$

4.

Expression	the terms in it	coefficient(s)	Constants
$6s + 9y$	$6s$ and $9y$	6, 9	none
$70p$	$70p$	70	none
$13x + 4$	$13x$	13	4

Skills Review 25, p. 31

1. a. the upper   b. the lower

2.

a. $153,270 - 46 \times 2,267$	b. $68,961 \div 543$
Estimation: $150,000 - 50 \times 2,000 = 50,000$	Estimation: $70,000 \div 500 = 140$
Exact: $153,270 - 46 \times 2,267 = 48,988$	Exact: $68,961 \div 543 = 127$
Error of estimation: 1,012	Error of estimation: 13

3. a. $2.64 \div 6 = 0.44$; $6 \times 0.44 = 2.64$
   b. $4.88 \div 22 \approx 0.222$; $22 \times 0.222 = 4.884$ which is close to the original dividend, 4.88.
   c. $7 \div 4 = 1.75$; $4 \times 1.75 = 7$

4.

t (minutes)	0	1	2	3	4	5
w (words)	0	40	80	120	160	200

c. $w = 40t$

d. t is the independent variable.

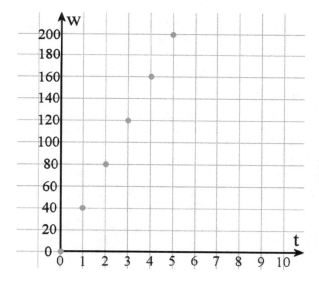

Skills Review 26, p. 32

1. a. 3,293.17   b. 54.05   c. 5,250   d. 3,809.58

2. The whole bag of pretzels contains <u>42.3 grams of fat</u>.
   First, find how many servings are in the bag: $282 \div 30 = 9.4$ servings. Next, multiply
   the number of servings by the amount of fat in one serving: $9.4 \times 4.5 = 42.3$.

3. a. y^4 b. $8x^2$
   c. $70p$ d. $3xy$

4. a. $(8.3 - 5.9) \times 7 = 16.8$ or $7(8.3 - 5.9) = 16.8$
   b. $(4a)^3 = 64a^3$
   c. $5(9 - 3) + 9(8 + 7) = 165$

5.

a. 6 cm = 6/100 m = 0.06 m	b. 4 cg = 4/100 g = 0.04 g
8 mm = 8/1000 m = 0.008 m	7 ml = 7/1000 L = 0.007 L

Puzzle Corner:

   a. $378 + 2 \times 165 = 395 + 313 = 708$ b. $735 \times 200 = 20 \times 7,350 = 147,000$

Skills Review 27, p. 33

1. a. $18x + 12 = 6(3x + 2)$ b. $21x + 7z + 42 = 7(3x + z + 6)$

2.

a.	b.	c.	d.
65 cm = 25.59 in	9.4 m = 30.84 ft	7.8 L = 8.25 qt	0.927 kg = 2.04 lb

3. a. 267   b. 168   c. 55

4. a. Kyle rides his bike eight miles in 30 minutes. He rides four miles in 15 minutes.
   b. Using the answers from (a), we can find that Kyle needs 45 minutes to ride 12 miles. So, he needs to leave home at 7:10.

5.

a. $\dfrac{40,051}{10,000} = 4\dfrac{51}{10,000}$	b. $\dfrac{2,069}{100} = 20\dfrac{69}{100}$
c. $\dfrac{72,069,183}{10,000,000} = 7\dfrac{2,069,183}{10,000,000}$	d. $\dfrac{140,317}{1,000} = 140\dfrac{317}{1,000}$

6.

Statement	Equation
a. The quotient is 9, the divisor is _12_, the dividend is 108.	$108 \div 12 = 9$
b. The subtrahend is 67, the difference is 34, and the minuend is _101_.	$101 - 67 = 34$
c. The factors are 4, 9, and _5_, and the product is 180.	$4 \times 9 \times 5 = 180$

17

Chapter 4: Ratios

Skills Review 28, p. 34

1.

a. $0.0009 \times 10^7 = 9,000$	
b. $10,000 \times 0.28 = 2,800$	
c. $\dfrac{21}{1,000} = 0.021$	d. $\dfrac{6.9}{100} = 0.069$

2. a. 906,007   b. 8,002,050,030

3. a. There are four roses to six daisies, 4:6 = 2:3.
   b. The ratio of roses to all flowers is 4:10 = 2:5.
   c. The ratio of daises to all flowers is 6:10 = 3.5.

4.

5. Jared has $89.40 ÷ 3 × 2 = $59.60, and Louise has
   $59.60 ÷ 4 = $14.90. So, in total, Cheryl, Jared, and
   Louise have $89.40 + $59.60 + $14.90 = $163.90.

6. Each bag weighed (3,000 g − 300 g) ÷ 4 = 675 grams.

7. a. $3 \times 8 + 19 = 24 + 19 = 43$ b. $\dfrac{1}{4} \times 1,200 = 300$

Skills Review 29, p. 35

1. Answers will vary. Please check the student's work. For example: $\dfrac{3x}{7} = 6$ or $x^2 - 75 = 121$ or $x + 62 = 76$.

2.

a. $\dfrac{200}{5} - \dfrac{40}{5} = 40 - 8 = 32$	b. $\dfrac{480}{8} + \dfrac{32}{8} - \dfrac{8}{8} = 60 + 4 - 1 = 63$	c. $\dfrac{18\ ft}{6} + \dfrac{9\ in}{6} = 3\ ft\ 1.5\ in$

3. a. 545.93077   b. 27.231538

4.

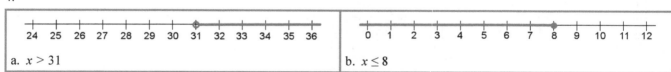

a. $x > 31$ b. $x \le 8$

5. a. 550 miles / hour   b. 3 yards of fabric per dress

6. a. $6^5 = 7,776$ b. $8^4 = 4,096$ c. $400^2 = 160,000$ d. $15^3 = 3,375$

7. a. 0.5 lb   b. 118.4 oz   c. 6.19 lb

Skills Review 30, p. 36

1. a. $x = 4.7$ b. $x = 0.32$

2. $\dfrac{\$96}{8\ hours} = \dfrac{\$12}{1\ hour} = \dfrac{\$144}{12\ hours}$

3. a. $y + 19$ b. $x - \$8$

4. Estimate: $7.5 + 5 - 9.3 = 3.2$ Exact: 3.2259

Skills Review 31, p. 37

1. a. 0.05 m   b. 0.003 g   c. 0.016 L

2.

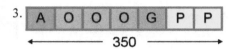

m (minutes)	0	1	2	3	4	5	6
w (words)	0	300	600	900	1200	1500	1800

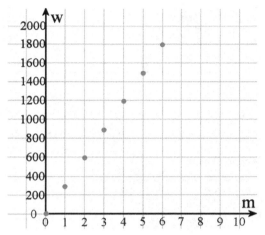

c. $w = 300m$ (or $m = w/300$)

d. m is the independent variable.

3.

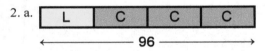

a. Bottles of pineapple juice (P) are in a ratio of 2:7 to all the bottles of juice sold.
b. For every 350 bottles of juice sold, there would be 50 bottles of apple juice, 150 bottles
of orange juice, 50 bottles of grape juice, and 100 bottles of pineapple juice.

4.

a. $0.900 \div 0.003 = 300$ $300 \times 0.003 = 0.900 = 0.9$	b. $0.50 \div 0.01 = 50$ $50 \times 0.01 = 0.50 = 0.5$	c. $0.0400 \div 0.0002 = 200$ $200 \times 0.0002 = 0.0400 = 0.04$

5. a. 640,000   b. 8,260,000

Skills Review 32, p. 38

1. a. <   b. >   c. >   d. >

2. a.

L	C	C	C

← —————— 96 —————— →

b. She baked 24 lemon cookies.
c. She baked 72 chocolate cookies.

3.

a. $(5 + 5)^4 \cdot (13 - 4)^2 = 810{,}000$	b. $90 + 50 \div 5 \cdot 7 - 3 = 157$	c. $\dfrac{6^2}{6} \cdot 6 = 36$

4.

Item and price	Unit price	What would this cost…?	
36 oz of cereal for $5.98	$0.17 per oz	8 oz of cereal	$1.36
20 lb of rice for $18.52	$0.93 per lb	3.5 lb of rice	$3.26
4 lb of beans for $5.22	$1.31 per lb	1.9 lb of beans	$2.49

5. a. $10a + 6 - 9x$ b. $2y + z + x + 7$

6. a. $x = 70$ b. $M = 900$ c. $y = 1{,}540$

19

Skills Review 33, p. 39

1.

a. $12(8c + 6a) = 12 \cdot 8c + 12 \cdot 6a = 96c + 72a$
b. $7(2 + 5a + 9b) = 7 \cdot 2 + 7 \cdot 5a + 7 \cdot 9b = 14 + 35a + 63b$
c. $p(x + 9) = p \cdot x + p \cdot 9 = px + 9p$

2. a. 85.649   b. 200.05307

3. The rectangle's width is 60 cm, and its height is 15 cm.

4. a. $3 \div 7 \approx 0.429$ b. $47 \div 12 \approx 3.917$ c. $91 \div 8 = 11.375$

Puzzle Corner:

36	–	19	=	17
–		+		(prime)
15	+	20	=	35
+		–		(multiple of 7)
43	+	21	=	64
=		=		(square number)
64		18		
(cube number)		(factor of 72)		

Skills Review 34, p. 40

1.

a. $83 \text{ in} = 83 \text{ in} \cdot 1 = 83 \text{ in} \cdot \dfrac{2.54 \text{ cm}}{1 \text{ in}} = 83 \cdot 2.54 \text{ cm} = 210.82 \text{ cm} \approx 210.8 \text{ cm}$
b. $78 \text{ km} = 78 \text{ km} \cdot 1 = 78 \text{ km} \cdot \dfrac{1 \text{ mi}}{1.6093 \text{ km}} = \dfrac{78 \text{ mi}}{1.6093} = 48.4682781333499 \text{ mi} \approx 48.5 \text{ mi}$

2. The length of each side is $4x$.

3. a. 0.000028   b. 0.0018   c. 0.015

4. They spent $390.76 in total.
First, divide to find the total amount of each discount for each set of luggage:
$169.95 ÷ 5 = $33.99 for the first, and $145.60 ÷ 8 = $18.20 for the second.
Then, subtract that amount from the original prices to find the discounted prices for each luggage:
$169.95 – $33.99 = $135.96 for the first, and $145.60 – $18.20 = $127.40 for the second.
Lastly, find the total cost that the family paid after the discount: 2 × $127.40 + $135.96 = $390.76.

5. a. 19/20 or 0.95   b. 5 3/100 or 5.03   c. 12 3/10 or 12.3   d. 1/100 or 0.01

Chapter 5: Percent

Skills Review 35, p. 41

1.

a. $0.0032 \times 100{,}000 = 320$		b. $100 \times 0.00714 = 0.714$	
c. $\dfrac{26}{1000} = 0.026$	d. $\dfrac{5.1}{100} = 0.051$	e. $\dfrac{803}{100} = 8.03$	f. $\dfrac{0.49}{10} = 0.049$

2. a.

    b. There are 8 triangles to 12 circles; 8:12 = 2:3.
    c. There are 20 shapes to 8 triangles; 20:8 = 5:2.

3.

a. $72\% = \dfrac{72}{100} = 0.72$	b. $4\% = \dfrac{4}{100} = 0.04$	c. $26\% = \dfrac{26}{100} = 0.26$

4. a. > b. < c. <

5.

numbers/letters	sum	difference	product	quotient
a. 27 and 3	30	24	81	9
b. p and y	$p + y$	$p - y$	py	$\dfrac{p}{y}$

6. a. 22, 31   b. 2, 5, 9

7. a. 0.73   b. 0.02005   c. 0.00608

Skills Review 36, p. 42

1. a. $1{,}000 - 560 = 440$ b. $(1/6) \times 42 - 5 = 7 - 5 = 2$ c. $12{,}000 \div 300 = 40$

2. a. Laura is walking at a rate of 84 meters per minute.
    b. It will take Laura 9 minutes to walk 756 meters.

3.

a.		b.		c.	
$5x + 2x = 62 - 13$		$8c - c = 3 \cdot 70$		$12x - 7x + 3x = 6 \cdot 80$	
$7x = 49$	$\div 7$	$7c = 210$	$\div 7$	$8x = 480$	$\div 8$
$x = 7$		$c = 30$		$x = 60$	

4. Of the 146 people who attended, $86/146 = 0.589... \approx 59\%$ were
    age 40 or older, and $60/146 = 0.410... \approx 41\%$ were younger.

5. a. $0.0864 < 0.417 < 0.9$ b. $2.638 < 2.68 < 2.836$

6.

a. 7.2 gal = 28.8 qt	c. 91 fl. oz. = 2.84 qt	e. 0.073 T = 146 lb
b. 8.5 qt = 272 fl. oz.	d. 638 qt = 159.5 gal	f. 5,600 lb = 2.8 T

Skills Review 37, p. 43

1.

a. $\dfrac{525 \text{ mi}}{7 \text{ hr}} = \dfrac{75 \text{ mi}}{1 \text{ hr}} = \dfrac{25 \text{ mi}}{20 \text{ min}} = \dfrac{50 \text{ mi}}{40 \text{ min}}$	b. $\dfrac{\$18}{45 \text{ min}} = \dfrac{\$6}{15 \text{ min}} = \dfrac{\$24}{1 \text{ hr}} = \dfrac{\$42}{1 \text{ hr } 45 \text{ min}}$

2.

a. 10% of 50 kg = 5 kg 30% of 50 kg = 15 kg	b. 10% of \$32 = \$3.20 40% of \$32 = \$12.80	c. 10% of 15 mi = 1.5 mi 60% of 15 mi = 9 mi

3.

a. $0.8 \times 0.07 = 0.056$ ↓ ↓ ↓ $\dfrac{8}{10} \times \dfrac{7}{100} = \dfrac{56}{1000}$	b. $0.006 \times 0.2 = 0.0012$ ↓ ↓ ↓ $\dfrac{6}{1000} \times \dfrac{2}{10} = \dfrac{12}{10,000}$	c. $0.015 \times 0.0003 = 0.0000045$ ↓ ↓ ↓ $\dfrac{15}{1000} \times \dfrac{3}{10,000} = \dfrac{45}{10,000,000}$

4. a. V = 4 in × 4 in × 4 in = 64 in^3 b. A = 9 cm × 9 cm = 81 cm^2

5.

a. $4(7 + p) = 4p + 28$	b. $5(x + 9) = 5x + 45$

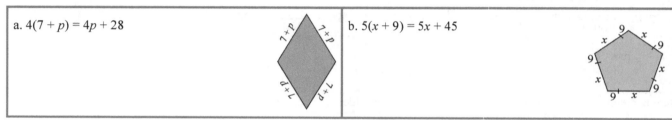

6. a. 341.49   b. 2,274.73

Skills Review 38, p. 44

1. $68 \cdot 45 = 60 \cdot 40 + 60 \cdot 5$
   $\qquad + 8 \cdot 40 + 8 \cdot 5$
   $\qquad = 2,400 + 300 + 320 + 40 = 3,060$

	60	8
40	2,400	320
5	300	40

2.

$148,516 - 12 \times 1,746$ Estimation: $150,000 - 10 \times 2,000 = 130,000$ Exact: $148,516 - 12 \times 1,746 = 127,564$ Error of estimation: 2,436

3. You can buy 21 pencils. You can reason it out like this, for example: Two pencils cost 30 cents. Therefore, with \$3, you can get 20 pencils. And with 25 cents, you can get one more, for a total of 21 pencils.

4. The ratio *turkeys : ducks : chickens* is 2 : 5 : 7, so there are 2 + 5 + 7 = 14 parts in total. If there are 45 ducks, since ducks make up 5 parts of the total, then one part consists of 45 ÷ 5 = 9 birds.
   a. The turkeys make up 2 parts of the total, so there are 18 of them.
   b. The chickens make up 7 parts of the total, so there are 63 of them.

5. a. \$2,888   b. 43.68 m   c. 2.418 kg

6. a. 19.8 hm

1	9.	8				
km	hm	dam	m	dm	cm	mm

b. 32 cl

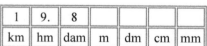

				3	2	
kl	hl	dal	l	dl	cl	ml

c. 19.8 hm = __198__ dam = __1,980__ m = __19,800__ dm
   32 cl = __3.2__ dl = __0.32__ l = __0.032__ dal

Skills Review 39, p. 45

1.

a. Discount amount: $5.20	b. Discount amount: $10.50	c. Discount amount: $32
Discounted price: $46.80	Discounted price: $24.50	Discounted price: $128

2. a. The aspect ratio is *width:length* = 1:4.
   b. The flower bed is 12 ft long and 3 ft wide.
   c. Its area is 36 ft^2.

3. a. $96x^5$ b. $45p - 18$

4.

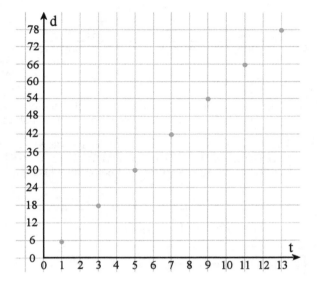

t (hours)	1	3	5	7	9	11	13
d (miles)	6	18	30	42	54	66	78

   c. $d = 6t$ (or $t = d/6$)

   d. t is the independent variable.

5. The average age is $12.4 \approx 12$ years.

Skills Review 40, p. 46

1. a. 116.058   b. 4.252

2. Alex picked 3 parts of the strawberries and Carl picked 5 parts. The two parts more that Carl picked consist of 26 strawberries, so one part would be 13. So Alex has $3 \times 13 = 39$ strawberries.

3. a. Mia washed $10/25 = 40/100$, which is 40% of her shirts.
   b. Only $8/40 = 2/10 = 20\%$ of the people drank coffee.

4. a. $7(12 - 9) + 5(11 + 8) = 21 + 95 = 116$

   b. $(132 - 24) \div 3^3$ or $\dfrac{132 - 24}{3^3} = \dfrac{108}{27} = 4$

5. a. $9x + 54 = 9(x + 6)$

   b. $6x - 24y + 36 = 6(x - 4y + 6)$

6. a. $8.46 = 8 \times 1 + 4 \times \dfrac{1}{10} + 6 \times \dfrac{1}{100}$

   b. $0.739 = 7 \times \dfrac{1}{10} + 3 \times \dfrac{1}{100} + 9 \times \dfrac{1}{1,000}$

   c. $52.1 = 5 \times 10 + 2 \times 1 + 1 \times \dfrac{1}{10}$

7. a. 7 cm = 2.76 in   b. 8.3 m = 27.23 ft   c. 5 L = 5.29 qt   d. 0.741 kg = 1.63 lb

23

1.

Number:	0.582631	9.317468
…three decimals	0.583	9.317
…four decimals	0.5826	9.3175
…five decimals	0.58263	9.31747

2.

a.	$\dfrac{50{,}262}{10{,}000} = 5\,\dfrac{262}{10{,}000}$	b.	$\dfrac{81{,}479{,}306}{10{,}000{,}000} = 8\,\dfrac{1{,}479{,}306}{10{,}000{,}000}$

3. $A = 32x^2 + 90x^2 + 16x^2 = 138x^2;\ \ P = 54x$

4. Sixty-five customers ate at the restaurant that day. Since 20% of the customers is 13, 100% of the customers would be 5 times that, or 65.

5. The original price of the first microscope was $168 ÷ 7 × 8 = $192, and the original price of the second microscope was $115 ÷ 5 × 6 = $138. So the two microscopes cost $192 + $138 = $330 in total before the discount.

6.

a. $129\ \text{oz} = 129\ \text{oz} \cdot 1 = 129\ \text{oz} \cdot \dfrac{28.35\ \text{g}}{1\ \text{oz}} = 129 \cdot 28.35\ \text{g} = 3{,}657.15\ \text{g} \approx 3{,}657.2\ \text{g}$

b. $35\ \text{mi} = 35\ \text{mi} \cdot 1 = 35\ \text{mi} \cdot \dfrac{1.6093\ \text{km}}{1\ \text{mi}} = 35 \cdot 1.6093\ \text{km} = 56.3255\ \text{km} \approx 56.2\ \text{km}$

Chapter 6: Prime Factorization, GFC, and LCM

Skills Review 42, p. 48

1.

a. $2^3 \times 31$	b. $3 \times 5 \times 11$	c. $2^3 \times 3 \times 13$

2.

a. $0.073 < 0.09 < 0.37$	b. $5.028 < 5.208 < 5.280$

3. a. $5s + 8$ b. $6y - 7$ c. $\dfrac{w^4}{w-2}$ d. $(9 - m)^2$

4. a. 0.29   b. 8,612.7   c. 0.3062

5.

a. 4 lb and 12 oz	b. 7 m and 21 cm
$\dfrac{4 \text{ lb}}{12 \text{ oz}} = \dfrac{64 \text{ oz}}{12 \text{ oz}} = \dfrac{64}{12} = \dfrac{16}{3}$	$\dfrac{7 \text{ m}}{21 \text{ cm}} = \dfrac{700 \text{ cm}}{21 \text{ cm}} = \dfrac{700}{21} = \dfrac{100}{3}$

6.

a. $\dfrac{6}{10} = \dfrac{60}{100} = 60\%$	b. $\dfrac{9}{20} = \dfrac{45}{100} = 45\%$	c. $\dfrac{8}{25} = \dfrac{32}{100} = 32\%$

Skills Review 43, p. 49

1.

a. 8 in = 0.67 ft	b. 17.3 ft = 207.6 in	c. 5 3/4 ft = 69 in

2. a. 15.311568   b. 548.88076

3. a. 12, 13, 14   b. 7, 8, 9

4. Of the 400 squares in the quilt, 60/400 = 15/100 = 15% were purple,
132/400 = 33/100 = 33% were yellow, and 208/400 = 52/100 = 52% were blue.

5. a. 55 miles per hour.
   b. 155 calories / ounce

6.

a. $\dfrac{1}{2}$	b. $\dfrac{5}{12}$	c. $\dfrac{2}{5}$

Skills Review 44, p. 50

1.

P	4	8	12	16	20	24	28	32	36	40
c	1	2	3	4	5	6	7	8	9	10

c. $P = 4c$ (or $c = P/4$)

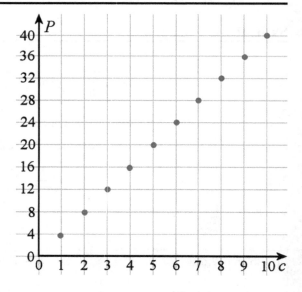

2. a. 4   b. 6

3. a. 0.06   b. 0.00189   c. 0.12   d. 0.0072

4. The camera cost $112.

5. a. $6,482 \div 7 = 926$ b. $55,260 \div 9 = 6,140$

Skills Review 45, p. 51

1.

a. 0.04×9
  4% of 9 = 0.36
	b. $0.22 \times \$700$
	  22% of $700 = $154
		c. 0.8×30 kg
		  80% of 30 kg = 24 kg

2. The ratio *lemon : orange : grapefruit* is 2 : 7 : 5, so there are 2 + 7 + 5 = 14 parts
   in total. If there are 12 lemon trees, since lemon trees make up 2 parts of the total,
   then one part consists of 12 ÷ 2 = 6 trees.
   a. The orchard contains a total of 14 parts or 14 × 6 = 84 trees.
   b. The orange trees make up 7 parts of the total, so there are 7 × 6 = 42 orange trees.
   c. The grapefruit trees make up 5 parts of the total, so there are 5 × 6 = 30 grapefruit trees.

3.

a. GCF of 18 and 30 is 6. $18 + 30 = 6 \cdot 3 + 6 \cdot 5 = 6(3 + 5)$
b. GCF of 72 and 48 is 24. $72 + 48 = 24(3 + 2)$

4.

Expression	The terms in it	Coefficient(s)	Constants
$3p^2y^5 - 17$	$3p^2y^5$ and 17	3	17
$\dfrac{9}{14}x$	$\dfrac{9}{14}x$	$\dfrac{9}{14}$	none

5. a. 74 km = 74,000 m   b. 15 ml = 0.015 L   c. 283 mg = 0.283 g

6.

a. $0.54 \div 0.09 = 6$
  $6 \times 0.09 = 0.54$
	b. $4.8 \div 0.8 = 6$
	  $6 \times 0.8 = 4.8$
		c. $0.096 \div 0.012 = 8$
		  $8 \times 0.012 = 0.096$

1. a. 37,052/10,000   b. 8,421,825/1,000,000   c. 59,430,176/10,000,000

2. a. Its area is 144 m^2.
   b. Its edge is 6 inches long.

3.

a. $59 + 72 \div 6 \cdot 8 - 37$ $= 59 + 96 - 37$ $= 118$	b. $\dfrac{9^2}{3^3} = \dfrac{81}{27} = 3$	c. $10^4 \cdot (60 + 80) \div 7$ $= 10{,}000 \cdot 140 \div 7$ $= 200{,}000$

4. a. She got 7 sections. 3 m ÷ 0.4 m = 7.5.
   b. She had 0.2 m of ribbon left.

5. a. The drone was discounted by <u>30%</u>.
      The discount itself was $48, and thus, the discount percentage is 48/160 = 3/10 = 30%.

   b. The 3-D puzzle was discounted by 25%.
      The discount itself was $26, and thus, the discount percentage is 26/104 = 1/4 = 25%.

6. a. The aspect ratio is *width:length* = 1:3.
   b. In terms of the aspect ratio of 1:3, the perimeter is 1 + 3 + 1 + 3 = 8 parts. If the perimeter
      measures 144 ft, then each part of the ratio is 144 ft ÷ 8 = 18 ft. So its width is 1 × 18 ft = 18 ft,
      and its length measures 3 × 18 ft = 54 ft.
   c. From the answer to part (b), its area is *width* × *length* = 18 ft × 54 ft = 972 ft^2.

7. a. 24   b. 36

Chapter 7: Fractions

Skills Review 47, p. 53

1.

a. $\dfrac{2}{9} + \dfrac{1}{6} + \dfrac{2}{5}$ $\downarrow \quad \downarrow \quad \downarrow$ $= \dfrac{20}{90} + \dfrac{15}{90} + \dfrac{36}{90} = \dfrac{71}{90}$	b. $\dfrac{11}{12} - \dfrac{1}{8} - \dfrac{1}{3}$ $\downarrow \quad \downarrow \quad \downarrow$ $= \dfrac{22}{24} - \dfrac{3}{24} - \dfrac{8}{24} = \dfrac{11}{24}$

2. Dana paid $97 and Mitch paid $152. To find how much Dana paid, subtract the $55 more that Mitch paid from the total cost and then divide by 2: ($249 − $55) ÷ 2 = $97. Then add $55 to the amount that Dana paid to get the amount that Mitch paid: $97 + $55 = $152.

3.

a. $3^2 \times 13$	b. 5×43	c. $2 \times 5 \times 37$

4. a. 0.75   b. 12.6   c. 4.629

Skills Review 48, p. 54

1.

a.	b.	c.
2 cm = 0.79 in 14.2 in = 36.07 cm	3 m = 3.28 yd 8.7 m = 28.54 ft	1 L = 1.06 qt 6.4 qt = 6.05 L

2. a. 3 1/10   b. 47/50   c. 4 29/140

3.

a. $4(8 + 12s) = 4 \cdot 8 + 4 \cdot 12s = 32 + 48s$	b. $9(5x + 7 + 3y) = 9 \cdot 5x + 9 \cdot 7 + 9 \cdot 3y = 45x + 63 + 27y$

4. a. 0.0915   b. 2.04013   c. 0.006238

5.

Number:	0.753824	2.6402769
…one decimal	0.8	2.6
…four decimals	0.7538	2.6403
…five decimals	0.75382	2.64028

6.

a. $\dfrac{9}{16}$	b. $\dfrac{1}{4}$	c. $\dfrac{3}{7}$

Skills Review 49, p. 55

1. a. 12   b. 8

2.

a. $\dfrac{3}{8} \times 4\dfrac{1}{6}$	b. $3\dfrac{4}{5} \times 5 \times \dfrac{1}{3}$
$= \dfrac{3}{8} \times \dfrac{25}{6} = \dfrac{25}{16} = 1\dfrac{9}{16}$	$= \dfrac{19}{5} \times \dfrac{5}{3} = \dfrac{19}{3} = 6\dfrac{1}{3}$

3.

a. 59 cm $= 59$ cm $\cdot 1 = 59$ cm $\cdot \dfrac{1 \text{ in}}{2.54 \text{ cm}} = \dfrac{59 \text{ in}}{2.54} = 23.22834645669291$ in ≈ 23.2 in
b. 27 kg $= 27$ kg $\cdot 1 = 27$ kg $\cdot \dfrac{2.2 \text{ lb}}{1 \text{ kg}} = 27 \cdot 2.2$ lb $= 59.4$ lb

4. a. $40x^2 - 12$ b. $7y + 9$

5.

a. $\dfrac{601}{6} = \dfrac{600+1}{6} = 100\dfrac{1}{6}$	b. $\dfrac{607}{3} = 202\dfrac{1}{3}$	c. $\dfrac{8,021}{4} = 2,005\dfrac{1}{4}$	d. $\dfrac{517}{5} = 103\dfrac{2}{5}$

6.

a. $80\% = \dfrac{80}{100} = 0.80$	b. $15\% = \dfrac{15}{100} = 0.15$	c. $4\% = \dfrac{4}{100} = 0.04$

Skills Review 50, p. 56

1. a. $18/138 \times 700 \approx 91$ people.
   b. $29/138 \times 700 \approx 147$ people.

2. a. There would be 21 puppies.
   b. There would be 105 puppies.

3. One pair of sports headphones costs $98.75 \div 5 = \$19.75$.
   Three pairs would cost $3 \times \$19.75 = \$59.25$.

4.

a. GCF of 84 and 60 is 12.
$84 + 60 = 12(7 + 5)$
b. GCF of 49 and 63 is 7.
$49 + 63 = 7(7 + 9)$

5.

a. $\dfrac{\overset{2}{\cancel{4}}}{\underset{3}{\cancel{6}}} \times \dfrac{\overset{3}{\cancel{6}}}{\underset{4}{\cancel{8}}} = \dfrac{6}{12} = \dfrac{1}{2}$
b. $\dfrac{\overset{3}{\cancel{9}}}{\underset{5}{\cancel{15}}} \times \dfrac{\overset{4}{\cancel{8}}}{\underset{5}{\cancel{10}}} = \dfrac{12}{25}$

Skills Review 51, p. 57

1. a. $8x$ b. $13p$

2. If the reciprocal is an improper fraction, the answer key lists it also as a mixed number

a. $\frac{11}{6}$ or $1\frac{5}{6}$	b. $\frac{7}{2}$ or $3\frac{1}{2}$	c. $\frac{9}{23}$	d. $\frac{1}{24}$	e. $\frac{4}{13}$
$\frac{11}{6} \times \frac{6}{11} = 1$	$\frac{7}{2} \times \frac{2}{7} = 1$	$\frac{9}{23} \times \frac{23}{9} = 1$	$24 \times \frac{1}{24} = 1$	$\frac{4}{13} \times \frac{13}{4} = 1$

3. Marlene got $850 in her pay check. If 70% is $595, then 10% is $595 ÷ 7 = $85.
   And 100% will 10 times that, or 10 × $85 = $850.

4. a. 100   b. 200

5. a. They pick 15 bushels of grapefruit per hour.
   b. They could pick 210 bushels in 14 hours.

6. a. >   b. =   c. >

7. a. 7,800,000 cl   b. 0.00135 kl   c. 49.3 L   d. 0.0652 dal

Skills Review 52, p. 58

1. a. 92   b. 7.88

2.

a. Each person gets 5/12 of a pie.	b. Each person gets 2/3 of a burrito.
$1\frac{8}{12} \div 4 = \frac{20}{12} \div 4 = \frac{5}{12}$	$1\frac{1}{3} \div 2 = \frac{4}{3} \div 2 = \frac{2}{3}$

3. Ed drove faster. Ken drove 440 ÷ 8 = 55 miles per hour,
   and Ed drove 325 ÷ 5 = 65 miles per hour.

4. a. Round $60.95 ≈ $60. Then calculate 40% of $60 = $24. The estimated discounted price is $60 − $24 = $36.
   b. Round $19.50 ≈ $20. Then calculate 18% of $20 = $3.60. The estimated discounted price is $20 − $3.60 = $16.40.
   Or round 18% to 20% and $19.50 to $20. Then calculate 20% of $20 = $4. The estimated discounted price is
   $20 − $4 = $16.

5. a. 365,000   b. 640,000,000

6.

Statement	Equation
a. The factors are 9, 5, and 7, and the product is <u>315</u>.	$9 \times 5 \times 7 = 315$
b. The addends are 24, 89, and <u>87</u>, and the sum is 200.	$24 + 89 + 87 = 200$

Skills Review 53, p. 59

1. a. 48.492   b. 5.073005

2. a. 36% (9/25 = 36/100)   b. 10% (8/80 = 10/100)

3. a. 5 × 9 + 17 = 62   b. 60 − (17 + 9) = 34

4. Since the 16 students that studied German make up two parts of the total, one part = 8 students.
   So, 5 × 8 = 40 students studied Spanish, 3 × 8 = 24 students studied French, and 1 × 8 = 8 students
   studied Chinese.

5. Each "1/4 of all" is 576 ÷ 4 = 144. The blue shaded area covers two of those sections of 1/4, so it is 288.
   Then, 1/8 of that is 288 ÷ 8 = 36. The unknown, x, is 7 × 36 = <u>252</u>.

6. a. 27,984 ft   b. 3.47 mi   c. 16,262.4 yd

1.

a. 3/5 of a number is 45. 1/5 of that number is 15. The number is 75.	b. 5/8 of a number is 60. 1/8 of that number is 12. The number is 96.	c. It is 132. 48 ÷ 4 = 12 gives us 1/11 of the number. Then, the number is 11 · 12 = 132.

2. a. The aspect ratio is *width*:*height* = 20:30 = <u>2:3</u>.
   b. The smaller painting's dimensions were 8″ by 12″.

3.

a. 20% of 70 kg = 14 kg	b. 60% of 40 kg = 24 kg	c. 1% of $50 = $0.50

4. a. 8.84 m   b. 6.56 yd   c. 0.84 lb   d. 6.86 L

5. Answers will vary. Please check the student's work. For example:
   a. Your purchase must cost less than $15.
   b. Students must be age 9 or older to qualify.
   c. You must spend more than $375 in order to be eligible to win a prize.

6. a. $x = 1.9 - 0.0072 = 1.8928$
   b. $x = 0.58307 + 1.30214 = 1.88521$
   c. $x = 3.0092 - 2.70914 = 0.30006$

Chapter 8: Integers

Skills Review 55, p. 61

1. a. $(300 - 50) \cdot (40 + 20) = 15{,}000$ b. $400 \div (60 - 10) \cdot 12 = 96$ c. $(70 + 80) \cdot 2 - 60 = 240$

2. a. $-\$67$ b. $+6{,}759$ m   c. $-6°C$

3. a. 12   b. 4.5   c. 0.07

4. a. \$703   b. 3.04 m   c. 5.695 kg

5. The number 1 makes the equation true: $\dfrac{1 + 8}{1 + 2} = 3$

6. The mower cost \$2,200. Earl and Matthew shared the cost in a ratio of 3:5, so there are $3 + 5 = 8$ parts in total. The \$550 more that Matthew paid makes up 2 of those parts, so one part would be $\$550 \div 2 = \$275$. Then, multiply that by 8 to get the total cost of the mower: $\$275 \times 8 = \$2{,}200$.

7. a. 3×83 b. $2 \times 3 \times 5^2$ c. $2^4 \times 3 \times 11$

Skills Review 56, p. 62

1. a. $h = 0.6 \times 0.04 = 0.024$ b. $z = 0.049 \div 7 = 0.007$ c. $d = 0.35 \div 0.5 = 0.7$

2. a. 3/4   b. 2/9   c. 1/2

3. a. $8(5a + 3) = 40a + 24$ b. $6(7x + 2y) = 42x + 12y$ c. $5(4x + 9 + 8y) = 20x + 45 + 40y$

4. a. The aquarium tank was discounted by 20%. (The discount amount is \$15, which is 15/75 = 1/5 of the original price.)
   b. The ham radio was discounted by 25%. (The discount amount is \$39, which is 39/156 = 1/4 of the original price.)

5. a. $\dfrac{7}{10} = \dfrac{70}{100} = 70\%$ b. $\dfrac{15}{25} = \dfrac{60}{100} = 60\%$ c. $\dfrac{19}{20} = \dfrac{95}{100} = 95\%$

6. a. The distance is 69 units. Add the absolute values of the y-coordinates: $42 + 27 = 69$.
   b. The distance is 19 units. Subtract the absolute values of the x-coordinates: $53 - 34 = 19$.

7. a. 0.427566   b. 3.74   c. 0.620

Skills Review 57, p. 63

1. a. $6 - 8 = {}^-2$	b. $^-4 - 2 = {}^-6$	c. $^-9 + 6 = {}^-3$	d. $^-2 + 5 = 3$

2. a. 21   b. 15

3. Forty-nine guests drank punch. If 30% of the guests drank coffee, then 70% drank punch, so we multiply: $0.70 \times 70 = 49$.

4. a. $6^5 = 7{,}776$	b. $11^4 = 14{,}641$	c. $9^6 = 531{,}441$

5. a. 93 ft $= 93$ ft $\cdot 1 = 93$ ft $\cdot \dfrac{0.3048 \text{ m}}{1 \text{ ft}} = 93 \cdot 0.3048$ m $= 28.3464$ m ≈ 28.3 m

   b. 47 L $= 47$ L $\cdot 1 = 47$ L $\cdot \dfrac{1 \text{ qt}}{0.946 \text{ L}} = \dfrac{47 \text{ qt}}{0.946} = 49.68287526427061$ qt ≈ 49.7 qt

6. Carl got an average of $50.4 \approx 50$ points per game.

7. a. $\dfrac{14}{63} + \dfrac{54}{63} + \dfrac{12}{63} = \dfrac{80}{63} = 1\,\dfrac{17}{63}$	b. $\dfrac{28}{30} - \dfrac{20}{30} - \dfrac{3}{30} = \dfrac{5}{30} = \dfrac{1}{6}$

Skills Review 58, p. 64

1.

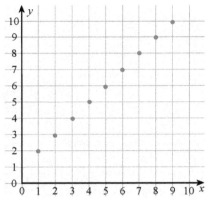

x	1	2	3	4	5	6	7	8	9
y	2	3	4	5	6	7	8	9	10

Equation: $y = x + 1$

2. a. $3{:}5 = 15{:}25$ b. $4{:}7 = 16{:}28$

3. a. The GCF of 27 and 72 is 9.	b. The GCF of 84 and 132 is 12.
$27x + 72 = 9(3x + 8)$	$84y + 132x = 12(7y + 11x)$

4. The company has 80 employees in total. We can find 1% of the employees by dividing: $68 \div 85 = 0.8$ persons. Then, 100% of the employees is $0.8 \times 100 = 80$ persons.

5. a. 0.088   b. 127.143

6. a. 2   b. −8

7. $(-5) + 4 = -1$

Skills Review 59, p. 65

1. a. $-7 - (-2) = -5$
   b. $-7 - (-5) = -2$

2. a. 9/10 or 0.9   b. 1/20 or 0.05   c. 7/50 or 0.14   d. 14 1/20 or 14.05

3. Please check the student's drawing. An example is on the right.
   Total area: _8_ · (_3_ + _5_)

   The areas of the two rectangles:

   _8 · 3_ and _8 · 5_

4. She had 1 19/24 cups of flour left.

5. He can type 975 words in 15 minutes. $780 \div 12 = 65$; $65 \times 15 = 975$.

6. a. 42   b. 80

7. a. not possible to simplify   b. $30a + 8y - 3$

Skills Review 60, p. 66

1. a. −4   b. −16   c. −11

2. a. 56   b. 15   c. 63   d. 36

3. a. Brad is 1.8 m tall.
   b. Mary's thumb is about 6.3 cm *or* 63 mm long.
   c. The car is 4.69 m *or* 46.9 dm long.
   d. My notebook is 19 cm *or* 0.19 m wide.

4. a. 3.047 < 3.407 < 34.07   b. 0.581 < 0.815 < 0.851

5.

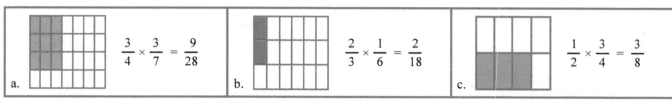

a. $\dfrac{3}{4} \times \dfrac{3}{7} = \dfrac{9}{28}$

b. $\dfrac{2}{3} \times \dfrac{1}{6} = \dfrac{2}{18}$

c. $\dfrac{1}{2} \times \dfrac{3}{4} = \dfrac{3}{8}$

6. She spent <u>70%</u> of the $150.
   She spent $150 − $45 = $105. That was 105/150 = 21/30 = 7/10 = 70% of what she had originally.

7. 3 ¼ pounds would cost $29.25. 3 ¼ × $9 = 3.25 × $9 = $29.25.

8.

a. 2.48 × 10 = 24.8 5.729 × 100 = 572.9	b. $\dfrac{63}{100} = 0.63$	c. $\dfrac{7.4}{1,000} = 0.0074$

Skills Review 61, p. 67

1. a. $4b$ b. $9a$

2. Norman drives 36 ¾ miles to work. Since the 24 ½ miles that Paul drives make up 2 parts of the total, then 1 part would be 12 ¼. The number of miles that Norman drives makes up 3 parts of the total, so we multiply 3 × 12 ¼ = 36 ¾ miles.

3.

x	−6	−5	−4	−3	−2	−1	0	1
y	−9	−8	−7	−6	−5	−4	−3	−2

x	2	3	4	5	6	7	8	9
y	−1	0	1	2	3	4	5	6

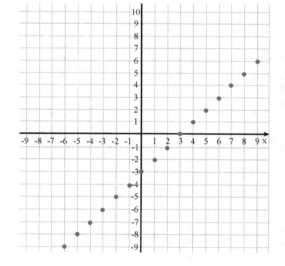

4.

a.	$\dfrac{72 \text{ mi}}{4 \text{ hr}} = \dfrac{18}{1 \text{ hr}} = \dfrac{9}{30 \text{ min}} = \dfrac{6}{20 \text{ min}}$	b.	$\dfrac{\$8}{15 \text{ min}} = \dfrac{\$24}{45 \text{ min}} = \dfrac{\$32}{1 \text{ hr}} = \dfrac{\$48}{1 \text{ hr } 30 \text{ min}}$

5. a. 0.955   b. 4,087.696   c. 0.65

6. a. $4.50   b. 6.15 m   c. 10.4 lb

Chapter 9: Geometry

Skills Review 62, p. 68

1.
> 297,428 − 12 × 7,249
> Estimation: 300,000 − 12 × 7,000 = 216,000
> Exact: 297,428 − 12 × 7,249 = 210,440
> Error of estimation: 5,560

2.

a. 0.7 × 30	b. 0.09 × $600	c. 0.05 × 8
70% of 30 = <u>21</u>	9% of $600 = <u>$54</u>	5% of 8 = <u>0.4</u>

3. a. $0.732 = 7 \times \dfrac{1}{10} + 3 \times \dfrac{1}{100} + 2 \times \dfrac{1}{1000}$

   b. $0.005163 = 5 \times \dfrac{1}{1,000} + 1 \times \dfrac{1}{10,000} + 6 \times \dfrac{1}{100,000} + 3 \times \dfrac{1}{1,000,000}$

4. a. The rectangle's aspect ratio is *width:height* = 8:3.
   b. The rectangle's aspect ratio is *width:height* = <u>1:6</u>.

5. a. 53 ft 9 in   b. 33 lb 6 oz

6. There are four such trapezoids, two basic ones and their mirror images:

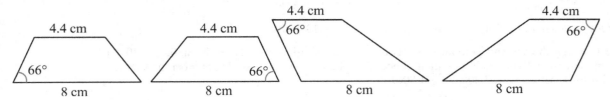

Skills Review 63, p. 69

1. The student's image may be a mirror image of this,
or appear rotated. The image is not to scale.

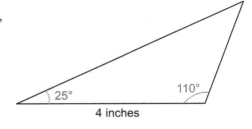

2.

a.	b.	c.	d.
0.42 ÷ 7 = 0.06	6.3 ÷ 0.9 = 7	0.024 ÷ 4 = 0.006	0.35 ÷ 0.05 = 7
0.06 × 7 = 0.42	0.9 × 7 = 6.3	0.006 × 4 = 0.024	0.05 × 7 = 0.35

3. a. Round $69 ≈ $70. Then calculate 35% of $70 = $24.50. The estimated discounted price is $70 − $24.50 = $45.50.
Or, round 35% to 40% and $69 to $70. Then calculate 40% of $70 = $28. The estimated discounted price
is $70 − $28 = $42.
   b. Round 18% to 20% and $364 to $360. Then calculate 20% of $360 = $72. The estimated discounted price
is $365 − $72 = $293.

4.

a. $120\% = \dfrac{120}{100} = 1.20$	b. $409\% = \dfrac{409}{100} = 4.09$	c. $13\% = \dfrac{13}{100} = 0.13$

5. a. 12/17   b. 1 1/35   c. 15/64

6. a. −6 < −2 < 0 < 1   b. −4 < −1 < 2 < 7

1. a. The student's image may be a mirror image of this, or appear rotated. The image is not to scale.

The area is: 4 cm × 2.3 cm ÷ 2 = 4.6 cm².

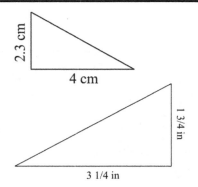

b. The area is 3 1/4 in × (1 3/4 in) ÷ 2 = 13/4 in × 7/4 in ÷ 2
= 91/16 in² ÷ 2 = 91/32 in² = 2 27/32 in².
Or, using decimals, 2.84375 in².

2.

Statement	Equation
a. The quotient is 7, the divisor is 9, the dividend is _63_.	63 ÷ 9 = 7
b. The subtrahend is _55_, the difference is 26, and the minuend is 81.	81 − 55 = 26

3. a. 0.37, 0.44, 0.51, 0.58, 0.65, 0.72, 0.79, 0.86, 0.93
   b. 4.165, 4.17, 4.175, 4.18, 4.185, 4.19, 4.195, 4.2, 4.205

4. Mitch spent more money (he actually spent 2 × 3/5 = 6/5 as much as what Eric did.)
First, find the price of the cheaper quadcopter: $295 ÷ 5 × 3 = $177.
Mitch spent 2 × $177 = $354. He spent $354 − $295 = $59 more than Eric.

5. Lisa's tomatoes weighed more. Her tomatoes weighed 6.1 × 2.2 = 13.42 lb.

6. a. Sonia didn't convert the percentage to the correct decimal. Her solution should have been: 0.40 × 30 = 12.
   b. Harold used the wrong divisor in his solution. Since 25% of a number is 1/4 of that number, he should have divided by 4 instead of 3: 7,200 ÷ 4 = 1,800.

1. a. 9   b. 3

2. a. 9 sq. units
   b. 20 sq. units
   c. 6 sq. units
   d. 12 sq. units

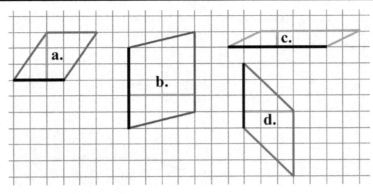

3. The root is 8: $8^2 + 27 - 4 \cdot 8 = 59$.

4. a. 0.518027   b. 26   c. 0.264

5. Mia originally had 30 stuffed animals. What she has left (18 stuffed animals) is 60% of the quantity that she originally had. So 10% of the stuffed animals is 3 and 100% of the stuffed animals is 30.

6. a. Carla: | C | C | C | C | C |

   Hannah: | H | H | H | H | H | H | H | H |

6. b. Carla: | C | C | C | C | C |

   Hannah: | H | H | H | H | H | H |

   c. Hannah has $144. Since Carla has $120, and the model has 5 "blocks" for her money, one block in the model is $120 ÷ 5 = $24. The model for Hannah shows now six blocks, which corresponds to 6 × $24 = $144.

7.

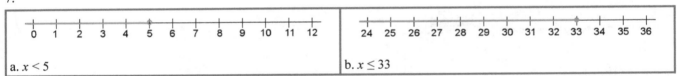

a. $x < 5$ b. $x \le 33$

37

1. Answers will vary. Check the student's answers. The image below shows some example triangles, where the base & altitude are either 2 & 9, 3 & 6, or 4 & 4.5 units. A triangle with base of 1 and height of 18 is also possible (drawn sideways).

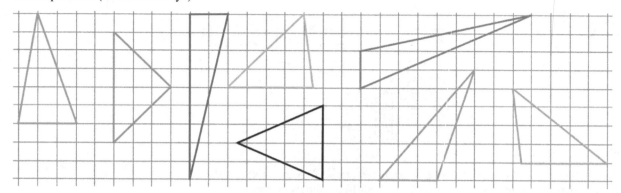

2. a. $(7.4 - 3.9) \cdot 5 = 17.5$ b. $(60 + 280) \div 4 = 85$ or $\dfrac{60 + 280}{4} = 85$ c. $(3 \cdot 2)^3 = 216$

3. a. $x + y + 14$ b. $2s + 6$

4.

a. $0.7 \times 0.06 = 0.042$	b. $0.005 \times 1.1 = 0.0055$	c. $1.2 \times 0.0008 = 0.00096$
$\dfrac{7}{10} \times \dfrac{6}{100} = \dfrac{42}{1000}$	$\dfrac{5}{1000} \times \dfrac{11}{10} = \dfrac{55}{10,000}$	$\dfrac{12}{10} \times \dfrac{8}{10,000} = \dfrac{96}{100,000}$

5. a. Answers will vary. For example: 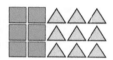 or
   b. 2:3

6. a. $5(7 + 10)$

   b.

7.

a. $\dfrac{3}{7} + \dfrac{5}{8} + \dfrac{1}{2}$	b. $\dfrac{11}{12} - \dfrac{1}{2} - \dfrac{2}{9}$
$= \dfrac{24}{56} + \dfrac{35}{56} + \dfrac{28}{56} = 1\dfrac{31}{56}$	$= \dfrac{33}{36} - \dfrac{18}{36} - \dfrac{8}{36} = \dfrac{7}{36}$

1. 6,600 cm^2. The parallelogram with base 110 cm and altitude 40 cm has an area of 110 cm × 40 cm = 4,400 cm^2.
   The triangle with a base of 110 cm and an altitude of 40 cm has an area of 110 cm × 40 cm ÷ 2 = 2,200 cm^2.
   In total, the area of the figure is 4,400 cm^2 + 2,200 cm^2 = 6,600 cm^2.

2. a. 65 miles per hour   b. $4 / pound

3. a. Answers will vary. Please check the student's answers. Example: 35, 70, 105, 140.
      The LCM of 7 and 5 is 35.
   b. Answers will vary. Please check the student's answers. Example: 24, 48, 72, 96.
      The LCM of 8 and 3 is 24.

4.

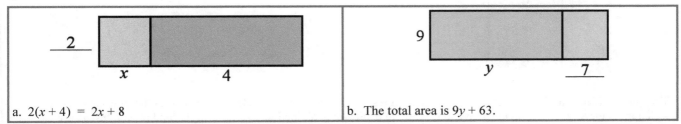

a. $2(x + 4) = 2x + 8$	b. The total area is $9y + 63$.

5. a. The distance is 81 units. Add the absolute values of the y-coordinates. 32 + 49 = 81.
   b. The distance is 46 units. Subtract the absolute values of the x-coordinates. 53 − 7 = 46.

6. Marilyn spent $20/$50 = 0.40 = 40% of her money, and Marcella spent $35/$50 = 0.70 = 70% of her money.

7. a. 0.090   b. 24.417

1.

a. $\dfrac{5}{12} \times \dfrac{2}{9} \times \dfrac{1}{4} = \dfrac{5}{216}$	b. $3\dfrac{1}{5} \times 6\dfrac{7}{8} = \dfrac{16}{5} \times \dfrac{55}{8} = \dfrac{2}{1} \times \dfrac{11}{1} = 22$

2. Answers will vary. Check the student's answer. For example:

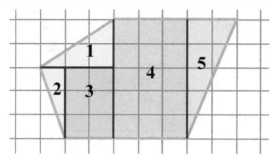

The general idea is to divide the pentagon into triangles, rectangles, and parallelograms − shapes that it is easy calculate their area. In the image above, the example pentagon is divided into *right* triangles and rectangles, as it is very easy to calculate the area of a right triangle using the units of the grid.

The total area consists of the areas of the five marked areas, and is $3 + 1.5 + 6 + 15 + 5 = 30.5$ square units.

3. Joel can cut 16 sections from the string ($5 \div 0.3 = 16.666...$). The section of string that he has left is 0.2 of a meter long.

4.

a. 10% of 70 kg = 7 kg	b. 30% of $25 = $7.50	c. 40% of 60 mi = 24 mi

5. a. $7^5 = 16,807$ b. $500^3 = 125,000,000$

6.

t (days)	1	2	3	4	5	6	7
b	150	300	450	600	750	900	1,050

c. $b = 150t$ or $t = \dfrac{b}{150}$.

d. t is the independent variable.

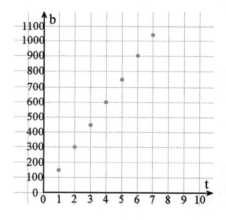

7.

a. 7.3 mi = 7.3 mi $\cdot$ 1 = 7.3 mi $\cdot \dfrac{1.6093 \text{ km}}{1 \text{ mi}}$ = 7.3 $\cdot$ 1.6093 km = 11.74789 km $\approx$ 11.7 km
b. 9 qt = 9 qt $\cdot$ 1 = 9 qt $\cdot \dfrac{0.946 \text{ L}}{1 \text{ qt}}$ = 9 $\cdot$ 0.946 L = 8.514 L $\approx$ 8.5 L

Skills Review 69, p. 78

1. a. >   b. <   c. =

2. a.

p	56	112	168	224	280	336	392	448	504	560
b	1	2	3	4	5	6	7	8	9	10

  b. $p = b \times 56$ (or $b = p \div 56$).

3. a. $^-10$ b. $^-3$ c. 50

4. 806,040

5. a. $\dfrac{2}{7} \div 6$	b. $\dfrac{7}{9} \div \dfrac{2}{11}$
$\downarrow\ \downarrow$	$\downarrow\ \downarrow$
$\dfrac{2}{7} \times \dfrac{1}{6} = \dfrac{2}{42} = \dfrac{1}{21}$	$\dfrac{7}{9} \times \dfrac{11}{2} = \dfrac{77}{18} = 4\dfrac{5}{18}$
This answer makes sense, since dividing a fairly small fraction by 6 should result in even a smaller fraction.	This makes sense, because 2/11, being a fairly small fraction, should fit several times into 7/9, which is fairly close to 1.

6. To find the area of the whole shape, divide it into three
rectangles, and find the area of each one separately.
Rectangle 1: 17 ft × 40 ft = 680 ft^2
Rectangle 2: 24 ft × 56 ft = 1,344 ft^2
Rectangle 3: 9 ft × 6 ft = 54 ft^2
In total, the area is 680 ft^2 + 1,344 ft^2 + 54 ft^2 = <u>2,078 ft^2</u>.

Perimeter = 212 ft.

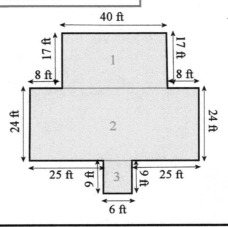

Skills Review 70, p. 79

1. a. trapezoid   b. rhombus   c. kite

2. One edge is 4 feet (4 × 4 × 4 = 64). So the surface area is: 6 faces × 4 feet × 4 feet = 96 square feet.

3. a. The distance between 7 and −12 is 19.	b. The distance between −3 and −14 is 11.
Subtraction: 7 − (−12) = 19	Subtraction: −3 − (−14) = 11

4. Joyce's pay check was $640 originally.

First find how much money she had before loaning money to her sister.
The $288 that she had after the loan was 3/4 of the money that she had
left after paying bills. So she had $288 ÷ 3 × 4 = $384 before the loan.
She had 3/5 of her pay check left after paying bills, so we calculate
$384 ÷ 3 × 5 = $640 to find how much her pay check was originally.

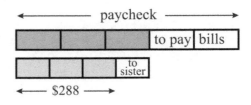

5.

a. $\dfrac{2,092,703}{10,000} = 209\dfrac{2703}{10,000}$	b. $\dfrac{405,168}{100,000} = 4\dfrac{5168}{100,000}$

6.

a. 2.7 ÷ 0.09	b. 4.8 ÷ 0.6	c. 100 ÷ 0.005
270 ÷ 9 = 30	48 ÷ 6 = 8	100,000 ÷ 5 = 20,000

7. $2^4 \times 3 \times 7$

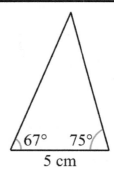

1. Check the student's image. The image here is not to scale:
   The student's image may be a mirror image of this, or rotated.

2. a. 0.26   b. 20.749   c. 5,231,760   d. 0.004713

3. a. $A = 50x^2$
   b. $A = 800$ cm^2
   c. $A = 3{,}200$ cm^2

4. The area in square *feet* is _5_ ft × _9_ ft = 45 ft^2.
   The area in square *inches* is _60_ in × _108_ in = 6,480 in^2.

5.

a. $-6 + (-3) = -9$ $\quad$ $7 + (-12) = -5$	b. $8 + (-8) = 0$ $\quad$ $-8 - (-6) = -2$	c. $10 - 13 = -3$ $\quad$ $6 + (-2) = 4$

6.

a. $\dfrac{5}{7} \div \dfrac{1}{4}$ $\quad\downarrow\quad\downarrow$ $\dfrac{5}{7} \times \dfrac{4}{1} = \dfrac{20}{7} = 2\dfrac{6}{7}$ Check: $\dfrac{20}{7} \times \dfrac{1}{4} = \dfrac{20}{28} = \dfrac{5}{7}$	b. $\dfrac{7}{8} \div \dfrac{3}{5}$ $\quad\downarrow\quad\downarrow$ $\dfrac{7}{8} \times \dfrac{5}{3} = \dfrac{35}{24} = 1\dfrac{11}{24}$ Check: $\dfrac{35}{24} \times \dfrac{3}{5} = \dfrac{105}{120} = \dfrac{7}{8}$	c. $1\dfrac{4}{5} \div \dfrac{2}{9}$ $\quad\downarrow\quad\downarrow$ $\dfrac{9}{5} \times \dfrac{9}{2} = \dfrac{81}{10} = 8\dfrac{1}{10}$ Check: $\dfrac{81}{10} \times \dfrac{2}{9} = \dfrac{9}{5} = 1\dfrac{4}{5}$

1. a. 1,950   b. 0.58

2. Answers will vary. Please check the student's answer.

3. a. The aspect ratio is *width*:*length* = 1:4.
   b. Its width is 12 ft and its length is 48 ft.
   c. Its area is 576 ft^2.

4.

a. $\frac{5200}{5} - \frac{80}{5} = 1{,}040 - 16 = 1{,}024$	b. $\frac{360}{9} + \frac{27}{9} - \frac{9}{9} = 40 + 3 - 1 = 42$	c. $\frac{24\ \text{L}}{6} + \frac{300\ \text{ml}}{6} = 4\ \text{L}\ 50\ \text{ml}$

5. a. 10 + 35 + 10 + 10.5 = 65.5 square units.
   b. 16 + 36 + 3 × 6 = 52 + 18 = 70 square units.

6.

 a. width = 1 in height = 3/2 in depth = 3/2 in 18 little cubes, each _1/8_ in^3 V = 18/8 or 2 1/4 in^3	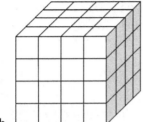 b. width = 4/3 in height = 4/3 in depth = 4/3 in 64 little cubes, each 1/27 in^3 V = 64/27 or 2 10/27 in^3	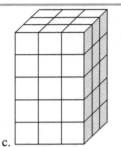 c. width = 3/4 in height = 5/4 in depth = 3/4 in 45 little cubes, each 1/64 in^3 V = 45/64 in^3

1. 20.5 in × 8.5 in × 12 in = 2,091 in³

2. a. $\frac{s}{4}$ b. $9m + 2.25n$

3. a. $240 + 75 = 315$
   b. $400 - 250 = 150$
   c. $4,200 - 600 = 3,600$

4. a.

O O O O O G G L L L L
← 264 →

   b. The ratio of lemons to all pieces of fruit is 4 : 11.
   c. There are 48 grapefruit in the display. $264 \div 11 = 24$; $24 \times 2 = 48$

5.

a. 4,000 g = 4 kg	b. 0.7 m = 7 dm	c. 0.9 L = 9 dl
600 L = 6 hl	0.05 L = 5 cl	0.003 g = 3 mg

6.

a. $7 - 17 = {}^-10$	b. ${}^-2 + 2 = 0$	c. $0 - 7 = {}^-7$	d. ${}^-3 + 11 = 8$

7. Answers will vary. Check the student's answers. The image below show some example parallelograms, where
   the base & altitude are either 4 & 5, 2 & 10, 8 & 2.5, or 6 & 3 1/3 units.

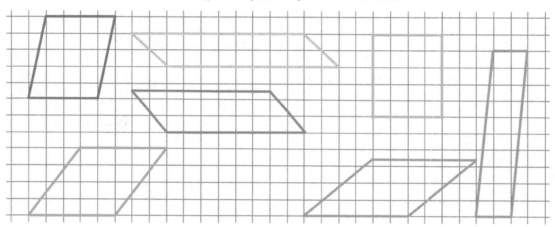

Chapter 10: Statistics

Skills Review 74, p. 86

1. a. $-12 < -9 < 0 < 3$ b. $-7 < -2 < 6 < 8$

2. Check the student's work. The altitude can be drawn in three different ways. Also, if you printed from the digital version, and used the "shrink to fit" or "print to fit" (or similar) option on the printer, instead of printing at 100%, the triangle will be smaller than intended, and the student's answer will be smaller than the one given below.

    Using the bottom side of the triangle as base, the altitude is 2.7 cm, and the area is 7.1 cm $\times$ 2.7 cm $\div$ 2 = 9.585 cm^2 $\approx$ 10 cm^2.

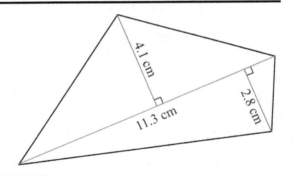

3. a. The distribution is asymmetrical.
   b. The peak is at 40 minutes.
   c. There are 20 observations.

4. a. 8   b. 15

5. Megan bought 14 plants. $35 \times 0.40 = 14$

6.

a. $\dfrac{70}{120} + \dfrac{75}{120} + \dfrac{24}{120} = \dfrac{169}{120} = 1\dfrac{49}{120}$	b. $\dfrac{110}{66} - \dfrac{11}{66} - \dfrac{6}{66} = \dfrac{93}{66} = 1\dfrac{27}{66} = 1\dfrac{9}{22}$

7.

a. 7 cups and 5 pints	b. 600 m and 2.8 km
$\dfrac{7 \text{ cups}}{5 \text{ pints}} = \dfrac{7 \text{ cups}}{10 \text{ cups}} = \dfrac{7}{10}$	$\dfrac{600 \text{ m}}{2.8 \text{ km}} = \dfrac{600 \text{ m}}{2,800 \text{ m}} = \dfrac{6}{28} = \dfrac{3}{14}$

Skills Review 75, p. 88

1. a. Median: 19   Mode: 18
   b. Mode: brown

2. The quadrilateral can be divided into two triangles by drawing one diagonal. This can be done in two different ways (two possible diagonals). One way is shown on the right. After that, one needs to draw an altitude to both triangles.

    The area is: 11.3 cm $\times$ 4.1 cm $\div$ 2 + 11.3 cm $\times$ 2.8 cm $\div$ 2
    = 23.165 cm^2 +15.82 cm^2 = 38.985 cm^2 $\approx$ 39 cm^2.

3.

a. $\dfrac{7}{7} \times \dfrac{4}{5} = \dfrac{28}{35}$	b. $\dfrac{4}{4} \times \dfrac{7}{8} = \dfrac{28}{32}$	c. $\dfrac{9}{9} \times \dfrac{5}{11} = \dfrac{45}{99}$

4. Randall will have read 245 pages in seven hours. $105 \div 3 \times 7 = 245$.

5. The coordinates of the original vertices were $(-5, 2)$, $(2, 4)$, $(6, 2)$, and $(-4, -2)$.

6. a. 30% of 50 kg = 15 kg   b. 10% of $25 = $2.50   c. 60% of 45 mi = 27 mi

7. a. Estimates will vary. Check the student's work. For example: the total cost was about $14 + $23 + $32 + $16 = $85.
   b. Exact cost: $84.95
      Error of estimation will vary according to the student's estimate in part (a). For the estimate given as an example for part (a), the error of estimation is $0.05.

1.

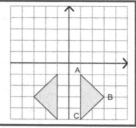

a. It is an isosceles right triangle.

b. See the image on the right.

c. 4 square units

2.

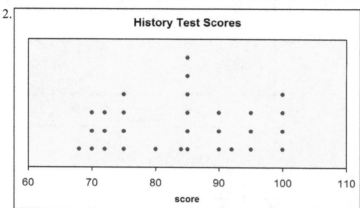

There are 30 observations.
This distribution has a large amount of spread.
The mean is 83.83. The median is 85. The mode is 85.
Any one of them could be used, though in this case, the mode
and median describe the peak of the distribution best.

3. a. 0.0108   b. 0.105

4. a. $8 + (-6) = 2$
   b. $-5 + (-12) = -17$
   c. $50 + (-13) = 37$

5.

a. $\dfrac{9}{4}$	b. $\dfrac{11}{8}$	c. $\dfrac{3}{14}$	d. $\dfrac{1}{24}$
$\dfrac{4}{9} \times \dfrac{9}{4} = 1$	$\dfrac{8}{11} \times \dfrac{11}{8} = 1$	$\dfrac{14}{3} \times \dfrac{3}{14} = 1$	$24 \times \dfrac{1}{24} = 1$

6.

a. $\dfrac{3 \text{ in}}{9 \text{ ft}} = \dfrac{1 \text{ in}}{3 \text{ ft}} = \dfrac{5 \text{ in}}{15 \text{ ft}} = \dfrac{7 \text{ in}}{21 \text{ ft}}$	b. $\dfrac{\$6}{15 \text{ min}} = \dfrac{\$2}{5 \text{ min}} = \dfrac{\$16}{40 \text{ min}} = \dfrac{\$32}{1 \text{ hr } 20 \text{ min}}$

7. a. 54   b. 300

1. a. $-9 + 4 = -5$ b. $0 - 6 = -6$

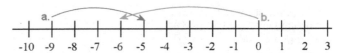

2. a. The aspect ratio is *width*:*height* = 4:5.
   b. Its area is 320 in². Since the picture frame's aspect ratio is 4:5, its perimeter
      is made up of $4 + 5 + 4 + 5 = 18$ parts. Each part is 72 in ÷ 18 = 4 in. So its
      width is 4×4 in = 16 in, and its height is 5×4 in = 20 in. Therefore, its area
      is 16 in × 20 in = 320 in².

3. Range: 7 grams. 1st quartile: 35 grams. Median: 37 grams. 3rd quartile: 40 grams.
   Interquartile range: 5 grams.

4. The shed's perimeter is 92 ft. Its area is 448 ft².
   The two sides are: 24×7 in = 168 in = 14 ft, and 24×16 in = 384 in = 32 ft.
   Then, the area is 14 ft × 32 ft = 448 sq ft. The perimeter is 14 ft + 14 ft + 32 ft + 32 ft = 92 ft.

5. She needs to make the recipe 2 1/2 times (40 ÷ 16 = 2 1/2).

> Granola – 40 servings
>
> 1 1/4 cup of coconut sugar
> 1 1/4 cup of molasses
> 5/8 cup of coconut oil
> 10 cups of oats
> 1 1/4 tsp of cinnamon
> 5/8 tsp of salt

6. a. 1/4   b. 3/40

7.

a. 0.4 × 90	b. 0.08 × $300
40% of 90 = 36	8% of $300 = $24

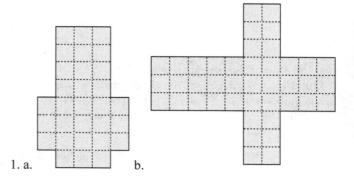

1. Check the student's work.
   The student's answer may be
   a rotated version of the nets
   on the right.

2. Answers will vary; check the student's answers.
   If you printed this from the digital version at
   100% (no scaling; no "print to fit"), then the
   student's answers should match the answers
   below fairly closely.

   1. a.   b.

   a. The width is 31 mm = 3.1 cm;
      the height is 18 mm = 1.8 cm
      Area: 560 mm² = 5.6 cm².

   b. Considering this as a parallelogram, the base is 20 mm = 2 cm and the altitude is 19 mm = 1.9 cm
      It is also possible to find the area by dividing it into two triangles, and finding their bases and altitudes.
      Area: 380 mm² = 3.8 cm².

   c. The base is 31 mm = 3.1 cm and the altitude is 15 mm = 1.5 cm.
      Area: 470 mm² = 4.7 cm².

3. a. Round $48.90 ≈ $50. Then calculate 40% of $50 = $20. The estimated
      discounted price is $50 − $20 = $30.
   b. Round 18% to 20% and $15.50 to $15. Then 20% of $15 is $3, and the
      estimated discounted price is $12.

4.

a. $-6 - (-8) = 2$ $\quad 4 + (-9) = -5$	b. $2 - (-7) = 9$ $\quad 3 - 5 = -2$	c. $-18 + 13 = -5$ $\quad -16 - 10 = -26$

5.

a. $6x = \dfrac{3}{5}$ $\quad x = \dfrac{3}{5} \div 6 = \dfrac{1}{10}$	b. $4x = \dfrac{1}{2}$ $\quad x = \dfrac{1}{2} \div 4 = \dfrac{1}{8}$

6. The bin width is $(37 - 9)/4 = 6.5 ≈ 7$.
   Starting the first bin at 9 will work.
   The subsequent bins will then start
   at 16, 23, and 30.

Price ($)	Frequency
9..15	6
16..22	10
23..29	7
30..37	3

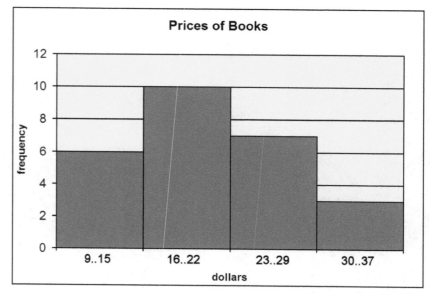

7. a. 14/70 = 2/10 = 20% of the children are girls.   b. 0.60 × 150 = 90 of the buttons are red.

1. The original price was $10,000. If 80% is $8,000, then 10%
   is $1,000, and 100% is 10 times that, or $10,000.

2. Minimum: 15 hours
   First quartile: 16.5 hours
   Median: 19 hours
   Third quartile: 21 hours
   Maximum: 25 hours

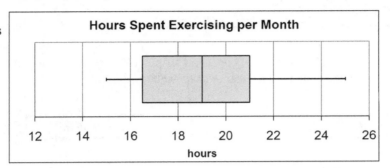

3. (i)

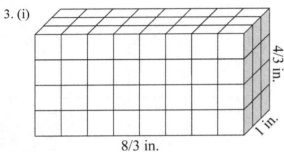

The model needs to be 8 by 3 by 4 blocks, but it can be in a different orientation from this picture.

(ii) There are 96 cubes.

(iii) One cube is 1/27 cubic inch. The total volume is $96 \times (1/27)$ in^3 = 96/27 in^3 = 32/9 in^3 = 3 5/9 in^3, which is the
same as you would get by multiplying the three dimensions, 8/3 in, 1 in, and 4/3 in.

4.

a. $-5 + 9 = 4$ $-2 - (-8) = 6$	b. $(-6) - 10 = -16$ $-4 + (-3) = -7$	c. $-12 - 7 = -19$ $(-9) + (-12) = -21$

5. Beth had 90 stickers originally, and Gwen had 60.

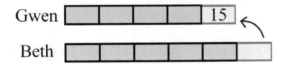

Drawing a model solves this problem easily. Gwen's and Beth's stickers are originally in a ratio of 4:6.
Since moving 15 stickers from Beth to Gwen makes them both have an equal amount, this 15 must be one "block"
in the model, and afterwards, both have 5 "blocks". Thus, Beth had originally $6 \times 15 = 90$ stickers.

6. a. 16.774   b. 5.375

1.

a. GCF of 18 and 26 is 2.	b. GCF of 45 and 75 is 15.
$18 + 26 = 2(9 + 13)$	$45 + 75 = 15(3 + 5)$

2. a. The volume of the gift box is 9,600 cm³.

   b. She fit 80 bars of soap in the box. The volume of one bar of soap is 120 cm³. So, we divide the volume of the gift box by the volume of one bar of soap: 9,600 cm³ ÷ 120 cm³ = 80.

3.

a. 25% of 60 kg = 15 kg	b. 75% of $28 = $21	c. 90% of 40 mi = 36 mi

4. a.

x	−4	−3	−2	−1	0	1	2	3
y	−7	−6	−5	−4	−3	−2	−1	0

   b.

x	4	5	6	7	8
y	1	2	3	4	5

5. a. $0.3 + 0.0426 − 0.039 = 0.3036$
   b. $0.74 + 0.0017 − 0.25 = 0.4917$

6. a.

Stem	Leaf
54	3 8
56	3 9
57	1 9
58	6
59	4 7
61	5
62	2
63	8

   b. The median weekly cost of groceries is $582.50.

   c. The first quartile is 566.
      The third quartile is 606.
      The interquartile range is $606 − 566 = 40$.

   d. The data is spread out a lot.

7.

a. 67 in $= 67$ in $\cdot 1 = 67$ in $\cdot \dfrac{2.54 \text{ cm}}{1 \text{ in}} = 67 \cdot 2.54$ cm $= 170.18$ cm ≈ 170.2 cm
b. 28 lb $= 28$ lb $\cdot 1 = 28$ lb $\cdot \dfrac{0.454 \text{ kg}}{1 \text{ lb}} = 28 \cdot 0.454$ kg $= 12.712$ kg ≈ 12.7 kg

CPSIA information can be obtained
at www.ICGtesting.com
Printed in the USA
JSHW020103160820
7253JS00003B/14